The Little Things

Ali S. Black

WestBow Press

P R E S S

A DIVISION OF THOMAS NELSON

WestBow Press books may be ordered through booksellers or by contacting:

WestBow Press
A Division of Thomas Nelson
1663 Liberty Drive
Bloomington, IN 47403
www.westbowpress.com
1-(866) 928-1240

ISBN: 978-1-4497-3685-9 (e)
ISBN: 978-1-4497-3686-6 (sc)

Library of Congress Control Number: 2012900314

Printed in the United States of America

WestBow Press rev. date:2/31/2012

"My grace is sufficient for you, for my power is made perfect in weakness." 2 Cor.12:9

ACKNOWLEDGMENTS

First and foremost, all my praise and thanksgiving goes to my heavenly Father and Lord and Savior Jesus Christ. His grace, forgiveness, and love that has been lavished upon me leaves me in amazement and wonder. His faithfulness to me has never wavered, even though times I have been unfaithful in my living and serving Him. Praise be to my Redeemer for his steadfast love!

The Lord has also blessed me with a godly, faithful, patient, and loving husband. God knew I would need a very strong man to stick with me through the ups and downs. Thank you to my hubby for never giving up on me.

No words can fully express my gratitude to my Lord for the precious gift of my son. I love my amazing son with all my being—don't know how else to put it. It is an absolute privilege and honor to be his mom.

To my husband and son, I am writing this to put an end finally to the pain and stop its cycle so it doesn't continue. This book is my way of allowing God, through my brutal honesty, to bring good out of what the Devil meant for death and destruction and shed light on the darkness. I pray that God will bless you with the ability to understand and forgive.

Thank you, Mom, for being understanding and encouraging me to do whatever I needed to heal. For your selflessness, I am eternally grateful. Your support of me through this process has been a tremendous gift to me. I love you.

Far too many others have touched my life to thank individually. The Lord has richly blessed me with loving and caring people who pray for me, guide me, and lift me up. The Lord has shown His love to me by surrounding me with those who have helped me through my journey, gently encouraging me along the way.

Lastly, thank you to my family. Even though my path in life has taken me through some dark places, it has made me the person I am today. I believe that if I hadn't traveled those roads, I would not have the empathy for others I have now. It's that empathetic quality I've come to appreciate and value the most about myself.

Contents

Preface

For the past several years, a constant prayer of mine has been that what the Devil meant for death and destruction, God would use for good and his glory. Often I am awed and amazed at how God has blessed and honored that prayer. By no means am I a finished work, but still very much in progress. The Lord has been faithful to me even when I have turned my back on Him. Every time I fell, God in his love picked me up, dusted me off, dried my tears, and set my feet upon the rock once again.

Many years of soul searching, appointments with psychologists and counselors, and much needed time with God have provided a greater understanding of myself and how my mind works. However, I know there is much more God has yet to reveal to me about who I am and His love for me. The one thing I have come to know is that my need and desire for love and acceptance is still a stumbling block for me, even as a Christian. Even now, the Devil, the master of lies, can make me doubt God's love for me, especially when I know I have fallen short of living a godly life. But then the Bible reminds me in Romans 3:23, "For all have sinned and fall short of the glory of God and are justified freely by his grace through the redemption that came by Christ Jesus." One thing I am sure of is that I am grateful for "grace" and for all the dear people who have expressed God's unfailing love to me along my life's journey. May I be faithful in passing that love along to other hurting souls who need to know God loves them.

My prayer for this book is that the eyes of parents will be open to the pain they may cause their children through simple words or actions. There may also be people searching for the reason for their inner turmoil and pain who may find comfort in knowing they are not alone and there is "light at the end of this tunnel" called life.

Background

We've probably all heard the saying that it's the little things in life that make a difference. Usually upon hearing this, we think of positive things like a sunrise, a fragrant flower, a smile, or a kind word—little things that bring joy to our lives. In this book, I hope to show you also how profoundly the little negative things can send us spiraling down into a world of darkness and despair.

If my memory serves me, nothing extremely traumatic happened to me as a child, although I have lots of gray areas in my memory. To my knowledge, I was not physically abused. For years, however, I have questioned the possibility of sexual abuse, which would explain the nebulous gaps of my memory and some other difficulties I've experienced in my life. However, I have no concrete memories of anything like this happening.

I was raised in a two-parent household with all my physical needs met. Even so, I grew into a deeply sad and troubled person, although most people would have never known the pain I concealed within my heart. I became a master at hiding my true feelings and emotions. My parents tried their best to do right by their four children. We never wanted for food, shelter, or clothing and were generally cared for. Still, a deep sadness and profound darkness permeated my heart and soul. It took me years to break down the walls, or should I say towers, that I built around my heart enough that I was able to come to terms with the pain. Even still, God is revealing truths to me to help me understand my life's journey and heal me from it.

Not all my childhood memories are bad. There were many happy times, including having a mother who was playful and fun. But I will not be discussing the happier times in this book. This book is not meant to be an autobiography. The main focus of this book is to share how a life of inner turmoil and pain can start with the littlest of things.

CHAPTER ONE

Negative In, Negative Out

ADMITTEDLY, MY CHILDHOOD memories are foggy at best. My mind just seems to want to write off that chapter of my life. Among the earliest memories I have is of a picture-perfect scene, in the recesses of my mind, of the daycare I attended when I was about three. The clarity of this memory is in stark contrast to how blurry many of my other childhood recollections are. It makes me wonder why and how I can even recall something so vividly when I know that I couldn't have been much older than three or four. It's just another "little" memory, or is it? That question haunts me. This memory is of the office of that daycare. From what I recall, it would have been on the left side of the building. When you opened the door to step into the office, a fairly large desk sat slightly off to the left side. Large bookshelves lined the wall behind the desk, and a candy jar filled with black jelly beans sat on the shelf among the books. A faceless man (at least in my memory) would call to me to sit on his lap, and he'd let me reach into the candy jar to retrieve one of my favorite treats. That's all I remember, but I know it was a place I visited often. This could be as innocent as it sounds, but why do I even remember it at all? If I recall the room so vividly, why can't I remember the face of the lady who would bring me into the room? Why can't I recall the face of the man who was waiting there for me? These are questions to which I'm afraid I will never have the answers.

Another strange but vivid memory I have from my childhood years has to do with a nightmare I had time and time again. First of all, I don't recall any other nightmares or dreams that I've ever had. I can't even tell you what I dreamed about last night. This nightmare, however, I can still recall as though it just occurred.

After sharing this, I suspect your reaction will be something like, "What a bizarre nightmare to have. Why would one even remember such a crazy thing?" But remember, I do. In this nightmare, I'm awakened by a loud noise coming from the backyard. After searching for a window to peer out, I see a group of ape-like creatures dancing with flames around my beloved apple tree. When one catches sight of me watching, they all charge for the door to my house. I scream and run to hide, but no one in the house hears me. Where's my family? There's no one in the house to save me. Just as these ape-like creatures are about to capture me and set my house on fire, I wake up.

Bizarre in every way! Bizarre to dream of such strange things, but stranger yet to remember the nightmare forty years later. What does that nightmare mean? Does it mean anything at all? There have been times as an adult that while reading about Daniel in the Bible, I've asked myself, "What could he tell me about my dream?" Over the years, I've questioned the important keys that these two memories may hold. But just as often as I've questioned their possible importance, I've discounted them as childhood nonsense. All I am certain about is that they both leave me feeling very uneasy.

I also remember some of the battles my parents would get into. Somewhere back in the hazy corners of my mind, I can see my mother crying in her bedroom as my father is yelling. I see a little girl about the age of four wrapped around her mommy's leg. She's pulling at her mommy, tears streaming down her face, begging her to leave her daddy now. That was me, and that is, to my knowledge, the earliest memory I have of one of my parents' fights. It would not be the last time I begged my mom to leave my father. Of course, as an adult I know why she didn't, but as a child all I could see was the pain he caused her. Dad was never home much because his job would keep him away for days, sometimes weeks, at a time. When he was home, a household that was peaceful in his absence would now be filled with screaming. Peace became pain, and I blamed my dad for it.

I have only one memory of ever being spanked by my father. I think I was about three or four. I don't remember what the spanking was for, but I do remember yelling at him from the top of the stairs, "I hate you." Even though I don't recall any other spankings, I do recall how much I feared him. He had this way of looking at me that filled me with fear. Seeing the way he also tore into my brother taught me that I didn't want to be on his bad side.

I remember times my father was affectionate toward me, but even those memories have dark clouds over them. Honestly, I don't know if it's because there was anything negative to his affections or if my fear of him and resentment toward how he made my mommy cry have turned all my memories to one big clouded source of pain.

Fast-forward a few years later to a bright, sunny day and sounds of laughter and excitement as my brother, sisters, and I piled into the station wagon with my parents. We're heading off to have a fun-filled day at an amusement park. Not far down the road, maybe a mile or so, the happy sounds of excitement quieted as the sounds of anger started from the front of the car. Now, my dad is pulling off the road just down from the firehouse. My mom hastily leaps from the car before it even comes to a complete stop. We kids stay in the car as my dad gets out now to chase after her. They continue screaming at each other, and my dad hurls an insult at my mother, calling her a "fat elephant."

Let me pause there for a moment. Have you ever considered the impact words of anger have on kids who are listening? Here's what I learned from those words: Outward appearance means a lot regarding how we'll be treated. Of course, as an adult, I realize outward appearance and beauty should not dictate our worth, but that's what I learned from my father's constant attacks on my mother's outward appearance—and I do mean constant. In the misty crevices of my mind, I can recall many times insults such as these were hurled with the intent to hurt the one I loved, causing me to internalize much anger and resentment toward my father.

As a young child, I adored my mother. Since I viewed my father as a source of pain, I clung to my mom and always took her side. She was the one who was there for me, cared for me, and played with me. These were not the only fights my parents ever had. They fought whenever my dad was home. Even when they weren't screaming, they would still hurl insults at each other. Fighting seemed to be the only way they knew how to communicate with one another. Starting when I was very young, my mom would share information with me about arguments she'd had with my dad or even negative things going on with my siblings, explaining her side of the story, so to speak. I enjoyed the closeness I felt to my mom as we would talk. Although neither of us knew it at the time, these talks were causing me to choose sides. I chose her side, further distancing myself from my father. Bit by bit, argument by argument, I closed off my heart to my dad, totally and emotionally disconnecting myself from him.

My mother was also a source of a lot of confusion for me, although I'm convinced she had no idea how her words affected me. Sometimes I would say things to reassure my mom that I was on her side, and she would quickly reply, "You should be grateful for your father. He works hard to keep a roof over your head, food in your belly, and clothes on your back." She was just trying to be a good parent, teaching her child to respect her father. But my mom was the one parent I put my trust in and for whom I had great love and admiration. Now she was basically telling me that I was being ungrateful to my dad for taking her side. At least that's the way I internalized it. I was left feeling guilty for not loving my father more. Imagine the confusion that causes for a young child. The reason you don't accept the one parent is because he or she is causing pain for the other. Then the very one who is getting hurt tells you to be grateful for the one doing the hurting. That's how I viewed it as a child anyway. Never could I see the two sides of the story in my parents' conflicts. I could only see it as my father's fault. As a little girl, I also felt that if I showed any affection for my father at all, I would be betraying my mom in some way. Now my mom was telling me I was acting ungrateful toward my father for not appreciating him more. I definitely came to believe that no matter what I did or felt was wrong. I learned not to trust my feelings. My only desire as a child was to make my mommy happy. She seemed so sad, and I felt it was up to me to make her happy. When I couldn't do that, I felt as though I had failed. I began to feel it was my responsibility and duty to make everyone happy and fix the world's problems. You can imagine the depression that set in each time I realized I couldn't make everyone happy. This realization would fuel self-hatred over the years. By the time I had reached my teens, I wore the very weight of the world's problems on my shoulders. I felt it was up to me to fix everything, but I was painfully aware I couldn't. The overwhelming stress I placed on myself depressed me to the point where all I wanted to do was sleep and not wake up. When I was awake, I was plagued by frequent headaches, would get shooting pains throughout my body, and often experienced shortness of breath.

I looked forward to the trips my mom and I would take to town. Hanging out with my mom brought me joy. Still, I remember her often saying on those trips things like how her life would be better if she weren't with my father or making references to how life would be better with a different man. She didn't mean better in a sexual sense at all; it would be just a seemingly harmless passing comment that she may be happier somewhere else. These statements would come to haunt me later on in life, but at that time I would just wholeheartedly agree with her. At least, I felt very strongly that her life would be better without my father.

As the years went on, I became even more of a confidante for my mom. She not only shared her side of arguments with my dad, but also discussed problems with my aging siblings,which were five, seven, and eight years older than me. Parents, beware of how much information you share with your kids. In my case, the more my mom would share negative things with me, the more I felt responsible to fix them. As an adult, I now know my mother did not expect me to solve her problems or disappointments. As a child, however, I felt it was my duty. Each time I failed in fixing something, it would strip away another piece of self-worth. Not only did I act as mediator in my family, but every time my friends would fight, I'd believe it was up to me to fix things. I wasn't literally asked to mend issues, but in my mind I felt that responsibility. Again and again, I would be unsuccessful. Each time I'd fail, another chip of self-worth would be chiseled away. I would conclude that I had failed and believe I was a failure. Years and years of this thought pattern left me with no self-worth at all.

These "little things" built the early foundations: little fights, a little sharing of too much information, little criticisms. "Little" grew into big and bigger emotional unwellness.

CHAPTER TWO

The Big Move

UP TO THE age of ten, I doubt any of my inner pain was noticeable at all. Well, it may have been to my mother or siblings, but not to outsiders. The only tears that were shed usually were during the fights my parents would have. I do, however, recall being a fairly content child. Now though, looking back, I can see how some negative thought patterns were already taking root.

At the end of fourth grade, my parents decided to move the family into my dad's foster parents' home, which required a change of school districts. The farm was on the other side of the river, only several miles away—but across the river in a different state. It may as well have been in a different country as far as I was concerned. I was being torn away from all the things that brought joy to my life. I'd miss the beautiful lake I went swimming in, the big hill where I'd gone sledding, the ice cream shop I was allowed to ride my bike to and would play video games at, and my walks to the general store to buy my favorite candy. Most of all, I'd miss my cherished and trusted friends. Even as a child, I could comprehend that life as I knew it was about to come to an end. I feared the unknown and was not looking forward to this move at all.

My mom tried to find girls who would be in my new class with whom I could form friendships over the summer. She also tried to keep me in touch with my friends on the other side of the river. The few girls I met during that summer seemed nice, but I felt very awkward and uncomfortable. I was somewhat shy in accepting and warming up to them, which I'm sure came across as wanting nothing to do with them, which in turn was met with a feeling that they wanted nothing to do with me. My mom scheduled many play dates for me that summer to make the transition into a new school easier. She did what she could, but I was already very guarded as to whom I trusted. In my mind, these girls were not to be trusted.

Home life was chaotic at best; lots of work had to be done to turn the old farmhouse into our new home. One sister was leaving for college, and the other was entering her senior year in a school she wanted nothing to do with. My brother was just off doing his own thing. I felt very much alone. Because of the age difference between my siblings and me, sometimes I felt like an only child. Emotionally speaking, I started to draw inside myself in an attempt, I suppose, to protect myself from all the pain I felt. About that time, I also started to notice all my mother's insecurities. In occasional comments, she would refer to how people looked down on us—how we weren't accepted because we were outsiders, even though my dad had attended the same school I was now entering. She said that only made it worse because people in the area didn't like my dad. I bought into her way of thinking hook, line, and sinker. As an already insecure child, it was easy for me to accept that I was an outsider. I already felt that way in my heart. Looking back, I don't believe that was the case at all. I know now I made myself the outsider because of my inability to accept others. You can imagine how this way of thinking affected my ability to trust people and my friendships through the years. My favorite times were the ones I spent alone exploring the woods, which I did a lot. Surprisingly, I know I came across through the years as being very strong, confident, and outgoing. No doubt that outwardly I seemed quite happy and wore a smile on my face almost all the time. I had mastered the art of acting and concealing my secret pain. Once in English class, our assignment was to write a poem about a fellow classmate. One girl who I wasn't even that close with wrote a poem describing me. She said "A smile like the shining sun to hide the storm clouds within." Yes, that was definitely me alright. How did she know? Was it that obvious? This scared me a bit. I didn't want anyone really to know me. I wanted them to know only the façade I was portraying. I can recall trying to keep people at an even further distance so they could not see what was really going on inside of me. Allowing them to see me without my mask required trust. Trust did not come easy to me. It was easier to act the way I felt people wanted me to and would accept me for than to trust them to accept me for who I truly was.

Only a month or two into the start of fifth grade in this new school, problems emerged. Girls in my class started a club against me. Anyone who hated me could be a member. Wow, kids are cruel. Can you imagine the trust issues this presented? Looking back on it now, it was likely just a reaction to them not understanding my hesitation to let anyone close. I'm sure that didn't make it easy for them to like me. I did have a couple close girlfriends in this new school who were outsiders much like me. The club didn't last long to my knowledge, and I did try to make nice with everyone after that. That experience, however, put a deep-rooted scar on my heart, resulting in a complete lack of trust for every girl out there. Only now can I see how much of a scar that left on my heart and in my mind. To this day, I have a difficult time befriending women. It's still hard to trust that anyone's appreciation of me is genuine. Since I couldn't trust the girls back then, most of my friendships were with boys, which of course just made the girls hate me all the more. It's not that I trusted the boys any more than the girls—I did not! But it seemed to me that I didn't have to try so hard to be accepted or liked. I was a bit of a tomboy as it was, so somehow I just seemed to fit in with the guys better.

In an attempt to support me, my mother only served to validate my dislike for the people at this new school by confirming in my mind that they looked down on us. Home life was also becoming even more confusing and difficult to deal with. Dad was home even less due to work, and my siblings were never home much either. For the most part, it was just me and Mom. My loyalty toward her grew and grew, as did my dislike for my father. When he would call home and want to know what was going on in my life, I had a hard time even carrying on a conversation with him. I didn't want any part in talking with him. Every time he'd want to spend time with me, I would cringe even more. Again, my mom would tell me I was acting ungrateful. You know the speech: I should be grateful for the roof, the food, clothing, and such, once again compounding my guilt for not caring more about my father. So begrudgingly I would go with my dad. Sometimes we would go to the river to swim. He would often point out how wimpy I was for not wanting to swim to the big rock or swim down the rapids, compounding my already strong sense of not being good enough. Other times usually consisted of him taking me along to visit his friends, where I felt as though I was being paraded around for them to see, like some prized possession instead of a daughter to be loved, once again confirming in my mind that the only thing I had to offer was purely physical. Keep in mind that I already felt like a failure because I couldn't seem to correct anyone's hurts or problems. Quickly, I accepted that the only thing of value I had to offer—the only way to receive love—was through my outward beauty. What a very tragic thing to teach your daughter!

These times out with my dad then became an opportunity for him to ask me what my mom had been saying about him and share his side of the story. Now I was really being placed in the middle, forced into a mediator role that I never asked for or wanted any part of. The anger grew inside of me for being the dumping ground for all my parents' trash. I don't remember ever telling either parent how this made me feel. After all, I was frightened of my father, and I didn't want to cause my mother pain. By now, visible signs of depression were starting to show. At least to my mom they were. She would often ask me, "What's wrong?" pleading with me to share with her. I would not. The walls were already too high for a child my age to know how to break down. All I knew at that point was when I would badmouth my father, my mother would usually remind me to be grateful. I didn't want to hear that speech again. I also knew that my sharing would cause my mom great concern, and I didn't want to be a burden. Most importantly, I wanted to make my mom happy, not cause her pain. My belief as a child was that sharing about how I truly felt and what was truly going on in my life and my heart would upset my mom. No, I couldn't do that! *Got to keep it in. Got to act better so no one, including Mom, can see. Must make her happy. Must make others happy. Suck it in; don't let it out.* Those are the things my mind would say to me.

During any other time I spent with my dad, he would throw criticisms at me. I'm sure they were meant to be constructive, but I internalized them into a further attack on my already low self-esteem. Anything I could draw a sense of pride from he would turn into a teaching lesson. When we would play catch, he'd point out that I threw the ball like a girl or that I didn't put enough effort into catching the ball. In the morning as I was getting ready for school, he would drill me on math problems. If I'd get any wrong, he would laugh and say something sarcastic. If I got them all right, he'd say that I didn't answer them fast enough. Even going to an amusement park, which should have been fun, was just another place my dad would point out my failings. If I didn't want to go on a certain ride, he would poke fun at me, making me feel like a wimpy idiot, until reluctantly I would go on the ride, often then feeling sick to my stomach for the rest of the day. One morning, I was making breakfast for my grandfather, as I often did to help my mom out. In walked my father and asked, "What are you making?" As I replied scrambled eggs, he pointed out that I was doing it all wrong. He said, "You only have milk and eggs there. You should add a little pancake mix to bulk them up a bit. Isn't that right, Dad?" he turned to his father to ask. My grandfather, knowing that my dad was never wrong, just quickly agreed with him. One of my dad's favorite sayings was "I may not always be right but I'm never wrong." Hurt and embarrassed, I just left the room without uttering another word, leaving my dad to finish making the breakfast for my grandfather. Remember: "Children are to be seen not heard." My dad would often use that saying. I knew better than to say anything. Here was something I thought I had been doing right—something I could draw a little pride from—and my dad basically told me I was doing it all wrong. Nothing I ever did seemed to be good enough.

The only thing my dad was ever happy about and would often compliment me on were my looks, my hair, and the way I dressed, reaffirming that the only worth I had was based on my physical appearance. He'd always say, "No daughter of mine is ever going to have a belly larger than her chest," again teaching me the importance of outward beauty and how absolutely unacceptable I would be if I didn't have it. These beliefs manifested themselves in my life through the years, leaving me to feel as though I had no value if I couldn't get people to accept, or love, me for the only thing I felt I had to offer—my physical beauty. This way of thinking set the groundwork for very unhealthy thought processing and decision making in my later years. It also made me very obsessive about my appearance and weight, causing me to stress over any single pound I may have gained.

By this time, my relationship with my mom was changing too. The sadness and discontent with her life were growing. She was consumed with the work that needed to be done around the house and taking care of both my grandfathers, one of whom had severe dementia. I'm not saying she wasn't there for me, because she was, always making time to run me wherever I needed to go—piano, voice, soccer, or work. She always attended my concerts and home games, never making me feel like a burden at all for running her all around. On the other hand, I don't ever remember my dad attending one thing. Maybe it's because by this point it didn't matter to me whether he was there or not. Amazingly, I can't even remember if he attended my high school graduation. According to my mom, he was there. That, I guess, just shows how disconnected I was from him.

My mom could sense the distance growing between us, but it seemed we were both powerless to change it. She would try to get me to talk. I would only retreat further inside myself to hide.

CHAPTER THREE

Hurt-Filled Memories

SOMEWHERE AROUND THE age of ten, my grandmother, who also lived with us, passed away.

She walked with a cane, and we used to get into playful tug-of-war battles with it. Her company was enjoyed, and now she was gone. Her funeral was the first I remember being allowed to attend. I remember feeling sad but also uncomfortable in not knowing how to act at one. *Do I let the tears out or suck them in?* It was an open casket, and I remember following along as people paid their respects. When it was my turn, I just felt awkward and uncomfortable.

A year or so prior, one of my friends had lost a brother in a car accident. As I recall, I wasn't allowed to go to that funeral because of being too young. That had left me feeling sad because I'd adored him. He was my brother's age and was just a joy to be around. I felt also that I was letting my friend down not to be there to support her somehow. I spent a lot of time at her home with sleepovers and such. What was once a home very much filled with joy had become a place of much sorrow. One of the things his parents were filled with sadness over was the fact that they had wanted to bury their son with his class ring, but it had gone missing just a short time before his fatal car accident. They searched and searched but could not find it. Only a short time after his death, I was there playing outside and came across something shiny by their shed. As I reached down to pick up this shiny thing, I instantly realized that it was their beloved son's class ring. Joy and sorrow hit me at the same time, both equally strong. When I brought the ring to them, I could see the same joy and sorrow in their eyes. As they thanked me for finding it, the pain in their eyes was so great that I wasn't sure if I'd done a really good thing or if I had just intensified their pain. Every time I felt I caused someone pain I would internalize it as something I had done wrong, as a failure. This brought me great pain and sadness. It wasn't a long time after this happened that we moved, and my friendship faded away over the next couple years. I still think of them occasionally and wonder how they are.

After my grandmother's passing, life in the house had a heaviness to it. That's the best way I can describe it. My grandfather seemed to be just going through the motions of life. There was a hollowness there, an emptiness. Other than times I would make him breakfast, we didn't interact too much. My other grandfather who lived with us suffered from dementia, and it was hard to have any kind of relationship with him. Watching how the responsibility of caring for the two of them fell on my mother made me sad. Occasionally, I would try to do things to help, but more often I just wanted to escape the sadness, awkwardness, and uncomfortable feeling of it all, leaving my mom to shoulder their care entirely alone. I felt terrible for not helping more, but I just didn't know what to do or how to make it better.

Now my memory brings me to a gorgeous sunny day. I was somewhere around the age of twelve or thirteen. My mom came to me in a haste and said, "We're going for a hike." Now, for weeks, my mom had been watching my brother's every move. My sisters were both away at college, and my brother had distanced himself from the family, even building a tree house a couple hay fields away from the main house. That's where he spent most of his time at this point, even sleeping there, only coming home to eat meals and shower. Many different friends of his were starting to hang around the tree house, some who my mom had never seen before. She'd watch them as they'd go hiking back through the woods, raising her suspicions as to what was going on.

On this particular day, my brother wasn't around, so she decided we were going to take a hike to investigate what my brother had been up to. Not a very deep hike into the woods, we stumbled on a large patch of marijuana plants. My mom directed me to help her pull them all out by the roots. I'm not sure what we did with them after that; I seem to recall them being set on fire. What I do remember is hiking back out of there quickly and fleeing to the lower fields behind the barn to hide. My mom knew my brother would be very angry, and she wanted to keep me safe. I'm not sure what I was thinking then, but I do remember being scared. As we crouched down in the tall grasses of the lower field, the beauty and peacefulness of the day were shattered by the loud cracking of gunfire. After only a few shots, the peacefulness returned. After staying hidden for a while longer, we cautiously started our trek back to the house. Thinking back on that now, I recall the fear I had of my brother still being there and if he were, what he would do. When we arrived at the house, my brother was gone. Up to this point, I never remember seeing my brother angry. The gunfire must have just been his way of venting his frustration and anger. We never spoke of that incident again, but my anger—for once again being placed in the middle a battle that was not mine nor should have been mine—remained. My brother didn't stay at the house for long after that. I remember feeling I was to blame for that, too, because I helped my mom uproot all those plants. I started staying at the house less and less as well. Whenever my parents would fight, I'd try to leave the house without them knowing. I'd spend hours hiking around the woods or take off to a nearby friend's house. If I felt that I couldn't leave the house, I would hide in my closet. The closet was not a walk-in closet, but it was deep. My clothes hung in front and in the back of them was a hope chest I'd lay on top of and pretend that I had disappeared, which is what I wanted to do. Sometimes I'd even fall asleep there briefly, and I'd come out once the rage-filled voices had quieted down. My closet sanctuary worked quite well to bring me peace in a home filled with anger and chaos. To this day, being in a loud, chaotic room gives me the feeling of wanting to run and hide, even if the loud chaos is from joy and happiness. It just makes my skin crawl. Somewhere inside me is that child who wants to run to her closet sanctuary to escape the madness.

In the meantime, with surprising contrast, school and friendships were going quite well. I seemed to be starting to fit in, involving myself in many activities and making friends. Between the ages of eleven to about fourteen, I developed many friendships in my new school and also held on to one close friendship from the area I lived in prior to the move across the river. By now, both sisters were away at college and my brother was off living on his own too. I believe that's why my friendships at school truly finally started to flourish. It was important that I find an outlet somewhere, and this at least was a healthy one. I'd say I was happy other than a struggling relationship with my father and still having to deal with the fights between my parents. Looking back, I have many fond memories of school and friends in my tween years. I'm amazed now that I can remember being happy during those years, because by the time I graduated, all I could think of was the pain I was in and how much I needed to escape. The darkness of my inner turmoil had completely shaded any fond memories I'd once had.

On the outside, I would have appeared as a happy, well-adjusted kid, but future trouble was beginning to brew. I was starved for adult attention, especially adult attention from men. As a child between eleven and fourteen, I didn't understand why. This set a very dark foundation for what would follow in future years.

CHAPTER FOUR

Boy Crazy

Now came the teen years. Have you ever read how important a good father/daughter relationship is to that daughter's ability to have healthy relationships with other men? Well, if you have, I'm sure you've figured out that I was headed for a very dark slippery slope. One of the things that I've learned is that if a young girl does not have a good, loving relationship with her father, she will often go searching for that love and affirmation from other men. My life experiences would definitely back up that theory. Also, at this point, I felt that the only thing of value I had was based on my physical beauty, which I felt was the only way I could gain acceptance and love. Even at a young age I remember having this unquenchable need for the affection of men. I was drawn to them like a magnet, seeking whatever positive affirmation they would give me. Counselors through the years have told me that was because of the lack of love in my relationship with my father as well as a deficiency of self-worth and low self-esteem. As I grew, my need for attention and affirmation grew as well. This need only made me feel worse about myself, fueling self-hatred. I hated the fact that I longed for this attention. It made me feel dirty. Even though not having much of a Christian upbringing, I was aware of God and Christ and wanted their love and acceptance desperately. I used to have a plastic statue of Jesus. I don't know where I came across the statue, but I do recall many nights holding Him in tears begging for His love.

My desire for the affections of men or boys made me feel bad, wrong, and unclean. As much as I wanted their attention, I feared them. As much as their attention made me feel good, it equally made me feel bad. What a terrible paradox to be trapped in as a teenage girl, viewing men, desire, and even love as unclean and dirty. I also was troubled by my feeling that I had to please them and make them happy, which made me feel dirty inside and out. These mental battles and other triggers had always left me to question sexual abuse at a very young age that somehow I just suppressed to the point of not allowing myself to remember. By my late teens, I remember starting to question if anything had happened to me as a child. As an adult, I remember having those questions in my mind by my teens, so I'm quite certain nothing of that nature happened to me then. If anything like that had occurred, it would have had to have been when I was younger—likely before the age of ten. Even now, sometimes very dark, cloudy visions start to emerge, and I just shut them out again. Not trusting any memory but questioning where this distorted thinking that I must make men happy came from fueled my need for their acceptance. I have never been able to answer those questions fully. Either no sexual abuse occurred or the Lord has protected my mind from it. In either case, I have learned to heal from the things I do have knowledge of as well as the things I don't.

The whole dating scene for me started off quite normally. A few childhood crushes. A very brief boyfriend/girlfriend thing with the neighbor across the street that amounted to watching TV together, holding hands, and going to the Fourth of July celebration together. Then at the age of fourteen my heart was swept away by an adorable sixteen-year-old boy with overflowing confidence and the ability to make me laugh. Oh, how I adored him. As far as I was concerned, the sun rose and set because of him. He quickly became my world, and I was flying high, but only for a very brief moment in time. We didn't even date for that long. But this was my first inkling of love—the giddy, got-to-see-him, got-to-be-around-him kind of feeling. I felt that as long as I had him in my life, I mattered and I was of value. Then in just a moment, he was gone, and I felt as if my world came crashing down. What little self-worth I had left, went away with him. This was the first time I ever remember wanting to end my life. I remember walking down the long lane that led away from my house, soaked from the pouring rain, to the highway to look for the next car or truck I could throw myself in front of, raging at God, raging at life. I just wanted the pain to stop. Of course, that amount of pain was not caused by him. It came from years of little hurts building and building up to a boiling point, leaving me completely void of value. I thought I didn't matter to the world and it would be better off without me. I didn't even want to be part of the world because it held too much pain. This was not the only time I contemplated suicide, just the first. By God's grace, I made it through, although I'm not even sure how. I remember that time spent by the highway in the rain and can still feel those agonizing pains as if it were yesterday. Now the pain comes from looking back on that little girl and wanting to tell her it's okay. Just look up! Just look to the Lord! At that moment, I started placing fortresses around my heart to protect me from any pain, numbing my feelings so no one could ever hurt me again.

As time went on, I stuffed those hurts deep inside, not allowing myself to deal with the pain, going along as if I were fine. The turmoil and pain continued to build, and I didn't understand why I felt so lost and confused. Around this time my mother had started to take in foster children, troubled teens, and unwed teen moms. This limited the time she had for me. Not wanting to make things more difficult for her, I usually didn't discuss too much with her about my emotions or the turmoil I felt inside. Slowly the closeness I had with my mom as a child started to drift away. She had no idea I contemplated suicide at that tender age. She also had no idea how head over heals I was with the boy who had just broken my heart. I never shared those feelings with her. I never shared much of anything with her.

By this point, I was working and spending very little time at home. Not only was I starting to detach from home, but also from friendships at school as I had done when I first moved there in fifth grade. The relationships I had with my girlfriends suffered the most as I began not to trust them again. Looking back now I realize that there were a few factors that played into this. Old memories were starting to come back and take a negative toll on me once again.

One night coming back from a school ski trip, on an old clanky bus, dark as can be, a fellow classmate came over to sit in the seat adjacent to mine. She asked if we could talk. This girl was a very pretty and popular girl, the one girl out of any of them that I always had the deepest lack of trust and contempt for. She started off by asking me if I remembered the club in fifth grade. You know the one, the "Haters of Ali Club." I responded that, yes, of course I did. She went on to say that she was sorry for the role she played in that, she being the leader of the pack, in a manner of speaking. My reaction was to brush it off as if it were all fine and in the past and of no effect on me now. I acted as though nothing or no one could hurt me. I put on a real tough-guy, or should I say tough-gal, approach to this genuine apology. I accepted her apology and thanked her for opening up to me. It meant a great deal to me that she sought out my forgiveness. I truly wanted to forgive, but somehow all the pain from that time in my life came flooding back. Now I found myself starting to question every friendship that I had once again.

Overwhelming feelings of inferiority started to plague me. I bought into believing the things my mom used to say about the people in the area looking down on us. This feeling started a rebellion in my heart against allowing these people to hurt me. Gradually, I started to detach from all my girlfriends. The anger and pain continued to grow, and in my mind the area and its people were to blame. Now I was sixteen, driving and working on the other side of the river, the side where I lived until I was ten, the side I thought I remembered being happier, where I thought I was more accepted. So I withdrew myself emotionally out of my relationships and friendships with the kids (at least the girls) I went to school with. I'd spend much of my time at the places I hung out at as a small child before moving to this dreadful place, trying to reclaim a glimpse of peace somehow, always having then to return to the place of pain and anguish.

Again I found myself only wanting to hang out with the guys—only now the friendships with them were starting to change. No longer were they the completely innocent buddy-buddy relationships from the past. Now it seemed I was seeking out their attention as if my very life depended on it, as if their flirtations were a requirement in how I'd feel about myself and life in general.

This would be about the time in my life that unhealthy thought processing started turning into something far more dangerous. An addictive behavior was starting to take root. When most people think of an addiction, they think of a chemical dependency, such as being addicted to drugs or alcohol. In my case, my drugs of choice were attention, affirmation, and love. My understanding of love was warped too. In my mind, if a man desired me physically, it meant that he loved me. If he loved me, then it must mean I had value. The only problem was that when a man or boy was attracted to me, it usually meant one thing: sex. My addiction was not sexual. The very thought of sex scared me. It was an addiction to the excitement provided by the feeling of worth that the attention and affirmation of men provided me. Every time things would start to go too far regarding sex, I'd push away. Sometimes the guy would want nothing to do with me after that, but most of the time I'd want nothing more to do with him. Either way, the relationship would come to an end and so would the attention and affirmation I received from it. This always left me feeling hurt and confused, fueling the inner turmoil and hatred within myself, leaving me in need of someone else's attention to make me feel better about myself.

I had no idea what was going on with me. I didn't realize that I was caught in an addictive cycle: no self-worth led to seeking out self-worth through the attention of men led to self-hatred for my actions led to no self-worth. The cycle continued, leaving me feeling powerless to stop it. Not only did I feel riddled with guilt for my actions, but I also felt a loss for each person along the way. For each guy, I'd make up this fairy tale ending in my head like some Disney movie. I watched *Sleeping Beauty* hundreds of times. One of my jobs at the resort I worked at was actually putting that movie on for kids to see at night. I dreamed about my prince who was coming to save me, each time getting smacked in the face by reality. I started to develop the attitude that the prince's armor rusted and he had to put his mighty stallion down due to a broken leg. Each time a relationship ended, my self-worth would go right along with it.

I didn't realize that the years of "damaged emotions" and lack of self-worth were the fuel behind why I was hopping from one boy to the next seeking approval and acceptance. I have since read many books that have helped me understand myself and my life. *Border of Disorder*, by Cherry and Dan O'Neil, gave me great insight into the addictive pattern I seemed trapped in. They say in the book, "Disorders result when our ability to cope with the stresses of life is somehow overwhelmed." They continue to explain what an addiction attempts to accomplish: "It helps people avoid dealing constructively with time, avoid dealing with difficult feelings of fear, anger, bitterness, and self-hatred, avoid dealing constructively with negative self-image, avoid dealing realistically with relationship issues, and avoid dealing effectively with stress and stressors." Dan and Cherry O'Neil continue by saying that the "recurring theme in cases of addiction is that the addict is anesthetizing some emotional pain." Further: "The addict's behavior is a misguided attempt to cope with life, not an intentional act of rebellion." Looking back on my past, I can clearly identify that I was trapped in an addictive pattern. Back then I had no clue. Now I see I was searching for some way to cope with pain and self-contempt. I was trying to kill the pain. As a child, a teen, going through it, I did not know the complexities of what I was doing.

During my teen years I also started to drink alcohol. I didn't drink compulsively, but I would drink from time to time as a way to fit in or numb the pain I was experiencing. Either way, the drinking didn't help my problems; it just added to them by making me more vulnerable to letting my guard down, even the slightest bit, with the boys. This drinking was not an addiction. I certainly didn't drink every day or even every weekend. Drugs were never in the equation. I never tried any of them and never even had the desire to. I'm sure during all of this I still came across in a very intelligent, confident manner. My personality was also playful and fun—a lot like my mother's personality actually. Strangely enough that was not an act for me. My bubbly personality came quite naturally. Unfortunately, underneath it was a hurting little girl who desperately needed love.

I chased after that love, but I did so in all the wrong places. In some demented way I felt that if everyone, or should I say every guy, liked me, then I must be worth something, right? Wrong! I would be just left feeling dirty and of even less value. Understand that I was not having sex with these boys. Just the flirtations and desiring their affections left me feeling that way. Even the couple of "normal" dating relationships I had I managed to destroy. As much as I sought after love, it seemed that I just couldn't trust it. Up to this point, my life's experiences had taught me that love could not be trusted. Every time someone's love for me seemed genuine, I would flee from it, not only because I didn't trust the person but also because I didn't trust my own feelings. I had absolutely no love for myself, so it was very difficult for me to accept that someone could truly love me, even though that's what I desired the most.

If I felt I was getting too emotionally attached to a guy or he was getting too attached to me, I'd start doing things to make him realize that I wasn't worth his time, sabotaging the relationship in some way, because inwardly I felt that I didn't deserve him. Sometimes I'd even convince myself that his family didn't accept me or my family, literally making up all kinds of excuses to blame the end of the relationship on other than myself.

Somehow in the midst of the madness that was going on in my life, I did manage to develop a couple long-lasting friendships. One was with a guy I had actually dated for a while. There was a true sense of love and acceptance with him and his family. The other was with a co-worker of mine who just made me feel special and was a lot of fun to hang out with. He always took the time to listen to me and never expected anything physical from me. If it wasn't for their friendships, I may have spiraled even deeper into a dark hole. I attribute much of my well-being to them and even their parents over my troubled teen years. The one boy's mom showered love and sun-filled smiles on me. The other boy's father I somewhat worked for, and he made me feel competent and hard-working and as if I had something to offer other than physically. These were sources of well-being to me, teaching me that I had value. This makes me think of the saying "God will never give us more than we can handle." Looking back over my life, I understand how God protected me from myself. Even though I wasn't aware of His presence during my teenage years, He was there with me, keeping me from plunging too deeply into a path of destruction. He was gracious to place certain people in my life at times when I needed them most.

CHAPTER FIVE

A New Start

BY THE TIME I reached my senior year I was working around thirty hours per week and going to school only until about 10:20 a.m. I spent whole weekends at the resort I worked at, only going home to sleep on the weeknights, very much an independent and free spirit. I emotionally disconnected from my parents to the point that I didn't care if they fought or who was right or wrong.

Still, I remember one day a fight of theirs getting very heated. I left the house and went to a friend's place up the road. We decided to go shopping in a town about a thirty-minute drive away. She could tell I was upset, and we figured shopping would be a good way to blow off some steam. We headed off for an afternoon of fun. We got to the store, parked the car, and started walking across the parking lot. Suddenly, I felt shock and disbelief consuming me as I saw my father coming toward us in the parking lot. At first I tried to pretend I didn't see him. As he called after me, I stopped to see what he wanted. He was asking me what my mom had been saying about him and trying to tell me his side of the story. Anger welled up inside me. Years of dislike and disgust started boiling over inside until I finally found my voice. This was the first time I ever recall speaking up to my father in defense of my mom and me. I yelled at him for following me and for placing me in the middle. I told him to leave me alone and go away. I'm not sure if he responded at all.

The way I spoke up and didn't back down seemed to shock him. To my amazement, he left without displaying any anger at all, leaving me feeling somewhat victorious, although strangely sad at the same time. Instead of my father causing me pain, I had caused him pain. My feeling of victory was shrouded in guilt.

Eventually, graduation day came. My freedom day! At least that's what I thought. The plan was to leave all the pain behind. I felt that all I needed was a fresh, new start and I could leave all the hurt there. After graduation, I attended a few of my classmates' parties until about three o'clock in the morning. I went home, finished packing my car, and was on the road by 6 a.m., excited about my future. My parents were also moving to a different place about ninety minutes from where I was going. The night before, in the midst of graduation parties, I said goodbye to very few people. Even fewer knew that I was leaving town the next day for what would become my new home four hours away. In such a haste to leave, I didn't even get any sleep before hitting the road. I recall having to stop at least four times on my way to get coffee to stay awake for the long drive. That was more than twenty years ago, and I remember that drive as though it were yesterday. I thought my pain would stop now that I had gotten out. Unfortunately, what I didn't leave behind were my insecurities, my deeply wounded spirit, and my addictive patterns. Instead of leaving the pain, I left a part of myself behind—a part that years later I became desperate to get back.

It didn't take long before I started to flirt with anyone who made me feel desirable, once again jumping from interest in one person to the next, being careful not to let anyone too close to me emotionally. For the most part, the flirtations stayed fairly innocent for quite a period of time, providing me with enough attention to fuel my addiction to it.

With one person, the flirtations went too far. A much older construction worker who was doing renovations to the building where I worked showered me with compliments and attention for about two weeks. He wore me down into agreeing to meet him for a drink at a local bar, even though I wasn't even close to the legal drinking age. I still don't remember how things led from the bar to the back of a van, but now I was dazed and confused as to where I was and what was happening. All I knew was I wasn't where I belonged and I needed to get out. So I started crying and pleading with him to let me go. Amazingly, he did, but not before hurling insults at me and telling me that this was my fault. In my mind, I told myself that he was right, this was my fault. Even though I knew that he did not have intercourse with me, I still felt the guilt, shame, confusion, and complete filth that one would feel from being sexually assaulted. That incident at least taught me not to place myself in dangerous circumstances with people I didn't know. At least I learned a lesson for a while.

Sometime after settling into this new area, I decided to go back home for a visit. Even though the area held so much pain for me, I still felt the need to go back from time to time. There were usually a handful of people I'd visit, one being my brother, who still lived in the area. The other was my former boyfriend, "Red," and his mom, with whom I stayed during these visits. I'd also visit my dear friend M, who I used to work with. I adored my visits and can still remember how I'd be filled with so much excitement and anticipation on my way up there that I felt that I would burst. Red and I had remained close, and I loved his family as well. My friendship with M remained close also. He always proved himself as a faithful and trusted friend. His friendship was so important to me because he always made me feel loved and accepted without there having to be anything physical between us. The visits

were always too short, leaving me feeling very torn between two places. In the back of my mind, though, I would tell myself that Red was better off without me and that M would be too. Even though I loved my visits, the area still held too much pain for me to consider returning. Each time after returning to my new home, I'd try to disconnect with and forget about everything and everyone from my past, although I still sent letters to Red and M. Eventually, I settled into my new home, and visits back home became fewer and fewer.

While out driving around with a girlfriend, we stopped to say hello to another friend of hers from high school, "Al." The warmth of his personality struck me along with a smile that lit up the sky. He and I became inseparable for quite some time. This relationship lasted longer than any dating relationship I had before. My addictive pattern seemed to disappear, and I was fully devoted to him. His family made me feel instantly welcome and loved, and I fully loved them back. This was also the time that I started learning more about God's love for me. I started listening to a contemporary Christian radio station and began going to church with Al and his family. Eventually, though, my inner demons started to torment my mind. So many negative thoughts invaded my mind. I was terribly confused as to how I was feeling and why. It's taken about two decades for me to start understanding it all. The fact that I had started going to church was wonderful, but the Devil was fighting against it with all of his strength, reminding me of all my past sins, leaving me once again feeling of no value. *How could God love someone as evil as you?* the Devil whispered in my ear. Now that the self-hatred started creeping in again, I started pulling away emotionally from Al. Maybe it wasn't so much me pulling away as it was me pushing him away. I told myself that I wasn't worthy of all the love he and his family showered on me. These feelings led me to disconnect emotionally from him and his family. They could not love me enough because I had no love for myself. The inner hatred I felt refused to allow any love

in. Even at church, I could totally accept the fact that I needed a Savior, and I wanted a Savior desperately. Unfortunately, the Devil had such a strong hold on my mind that I couldn't accept that God could love someone like me.

Remember my trips to town with my mom and how she would question out loud how her life would be better with someone else? Now that question was playing over and over again in my head. Since I didn't understand the source of pain or even where the question in my mind was coming from, I started to think that I would be happier with someone else, blaming Al for my lack of happiness.

Now the groundwork for fueling that addictive behavior was starting to take root again. Once that self-hatred started creeping back in my mind, I was desperate to find something or someone who could make me feel better about myself. While I was still with Al, I could feel myself emotionally detaching from him and looking for attention, affirmation, and my warped understanding of love from other men. During this time I found someone who I thought could make me happier, so I broke things off with Al. I also stopped attending church. Instead of being happier, though, I felt even worse. I beat myself up mentally for the pain I afflicted on Al and realized that this new guy was not the answer to all my problems.

CHAPTER SIX

Longing for Love

ONCE AGAIN SEARCHING for love and acceptance, I found my way back to Al, who accepted me back without question. Again for a while his acceptance and love for me seemed to save me from my destructive self. We started attending a new church together. This church was like no church I had ever been to. First of all, it didn't even have a denominational title, which was strange and foreign to me. I recall being overwhelmed with how many people came over to welcome us. The most profound thing to me was that everyone wore smiles and seemed very happy to be there. At that point I knew I wanted what they had, although I had no idea how to get it. Something shined through them—a radiant, joyful glow—and I wanted it.

As a child, I would occasionally attend Sunday school class at a Methodist church that was less than a quarter-mile walk from my house. My parents and siblings didn't come along. I remember being fascinated by the Bible stories and loved singing the Bible songs, especially "Jesus Loves Me." When I would watch the adults, though, they always looked somber to me. No sign of joy at all. Then in my teens I would go to CYO (Catholic Youth Organization) meetings with my friends. I wasn't Catholic, but they were. The meetings were fun, but the masses were solemn. So I grew up learning about reverence for God but didn't really understand a thing about His love. My mom did, however, give me a glimmer of understanding about God's love for us. She loved to sing the hymns "The Old Rugged Cross" and "In the Garden." She would also tell me about a prayer she prayed as a child from her closet and how God answered that prayer. Still, I remember growing up feeling that God was to be feared. I mean literally a God to be afraid of. Not a God of love. A counselor once told me that some people tend to view their heavenly Father the way they view their earthly father. That made sense to me. No wonder why I was frightened of God; I was frightened of my earthly father. It was hard to see God as a God of love when I could not view my earthly father in that way.

Al and I attended this new church for quite a while. I remember many times asking Jesus into my heart, which gave me joy, but still I didn't seem to have inner peace. I just couldn't understand, if I was truly a child of God, why I was still struggling with a deep sense of inner pain and confusion. Why couldn't God just instantly make me a perfect person? Why was I still struggling with my sinful nature? The Devil would whisper to me that if I were a child of God, I would no longer be struggling with a sinful nature. As time went on, my unhappiness grew. My relationship with Al ended, and I stopped attending church on a regular basis once again.

For years, I tried to figure out what led to the breakup between Al and me in a desperate attempt to try to learn from it so I would not repeat it. Unfortunately, I just couldn't understand all the complexities at that time. To this day, I wish I had the chance to tell him I'm sorry for all the pain I put him through. It took me many years, even well into my marriage, to start coming to terms with what would happen in my mind regarding accepting love. It seemed to me that every time I'd find something resembling real love, I'd close off my heart to it, much the way I did with my father. I was so afraid of being hurt by the person I loved or who loved me that my subconscious would just decide to put up massive walls around my emotions again so no one could penetrate. The other factor that played in was my complete unwillingness to accept that anyone could truly love someone like me. Sadly, the one thing I needed most, love, was the one thing I couldn't seem to accept.

It didn't take long for me to fall back into the same patterns of searching for someone to love me and place worth and value in me. The problem was that the men who were all too willing to shower me with affection were not the trustworthy and loyal type and had many problems of their own. My addictive pattern started to take on a new twist. Now a codependency was taking root. Not only was I searching for someone to love me, but I was searching for someone to fix. I'd seek out men who I felt it was my responsibility to help in some way. Remember how as a child I felt it was up to me to fix everyone's problems? As an adult I was once again taking on that role. Only now I wasn't just trying to fix their problems; I was trying to fix them. Years later I would come to understand there was another driving force to this. I felt like such a failure for not being able to fix myself that I thought if only I could help someone else, then maybe I'd feel better—maybe in some way that would make me more valuable and acceptable in God's sight.

I got involved with a co-worker. He seemed so unhappy in his current dating situation. I felt as though it were up to me to make him happy. During our dating relationship, he was emotionally abusive. I just felt as if that's what I deserved. After dealing with the emotional abuse for months, I came to realize that not only was he in a relationship with me, but he never really ended his other one. Devastated, I tore out of his house and took off in my car. It was very late at night, actually well after midnight. The rain was coming down so hard I could barely see, especially since tears were flooding my eyes. The next thing I remember is approaching a bridge that went over a narrow river. Then the thought hit me: *Why don't I just drive off the bridge? It would look like an accident. No one would know.* Then another voice said, *Yes, but what if you don't die and just end up paralyzed or something?* The car managed to stay on the road and brought me safely home. Now after two o'clock in the morning, I was still dealing with suicidal thoughts. I called a friend, and she was able to calm me down and talk some sense into my head. It seemed that every time someone would reject me, it would just compound in my mind that I was worthless. This would send me into a very deep, desperate place of despair, leaving me to want to end my life to stop the pain.

God got my attention again and made me realize my need for Him in my life. I did start attending church, though not on a regular basis. Al was still going to the same church, and we managed to remain friends. I started to realize how disconnected I felt inside. Somehow the way I left my childhood home left me feeling like two different people in a way, Ali the young girl and Ali the young adult. There was such a separation between the two that I found myself desperately missing my youth and innocence. So I decided to go back home for a visit again. The relationships that once were so close with Red, his mom, and M were now changing. The closeness I once felt there had faded away. The visit was bittersweet, leaving me feeling that I didn't belong anywhere. During the week, I prayed for God to show me where I belonged. The entire week there it rained and was still raining the day I left. As I headed back to my new home, about halfway there the rain stopped. I was literally driving out of the storm. Behind me, all I could see were dark storm clouds, and in front of me, I could see the sun winning the battle through the clouds. Its rays were shining brightly. Immediately I recognized this as God's answer to me. He was saying to leave the storm clouds behind and follow the sun. After this,

I never thought of moving back home again. I'd occasionally return to visit my brother, but all other relationships in the area dissolved. The disconnection within myself and my past, however, remained, leaving me to feel much sorrow for the child I left behind, that child being me.

CHAPTER SEVEN

Broken Beyond Repair

I GOT BACK to my new home and somewhat resolved that things needed to change in my life. I longed to feel better about myself. I was going to church, but not understanding the gift of God's grace. I was still looking for love and acceptance, realizing that I needed to change where I looked for it, but totally missing the importance that it was God's love I needed to accept in my life. I wanted it but did not feel worthy of it. This was my mindset during the time I met my future husband.

I'm not going to go into detail about how we met. What I want to express is how I viewed him. He didn't fit the mold of the other men I would fall for. He didn't shower me with compliments and sweet talk that fed my addictive behavior. From what I could tell, he didn't seem broken. So I didn't have the sense that I needed to fix him. Up to this point I was drawn to men that I felt needed me to help fix them. Now I was trying to change my mindset. So I was looking to this man to somehow fix me. He came from a solid, loving family, he was trustworthy and great with kids, and he went to church with me. I felt safe and secure with him. I was sure he would save me from myself. Of course, he didn't realize that's how I viewed him. I'm quite certain that I didn't even realize that's what I was doing.

I have no doubt that he didn't see me as broken, even though that's how I had always felt deep inside, in the place where I wouldn't allow anyone to see. I had a very stable job for an amazingly supportive boss whom I adored. He was the kind of boss who made you feel like part of the team, capable, liked, and full of promise. He instilled value and purpose in me. I seemed and actually was ambitious and worked a second job just to have a bit of extra spending money. I attended church regularly, had many friends, was bubbly and friendly, and usually wore a smile. So how could my future husband possibly see that I was broken? How could anyone see? I didn't allow them to.

Very early on into our marriage, I began to realize that I didn't feel fixed. The day I said "I do" was not an instant cure to all my emotional problems. Actually, the opposite started to take place. I believed that marriage would fix or save me. When it didn't, I started to become angry and discontented. Every unkind word from my husband, even if said as a joke, would emotionally throw me back to my childhood, where I'd remember unkind words my father would say to my mother or me. Anger toward God brewed within me; I blamed God for my unhappiness. Then I'd feel ashamed for my anger and felt as though God couldn't possibly ever accept someone like me. I just couldn't internalize the fact that "there is therefore now no condemnation for those in Christ Jesus" (Rom. 8:1). I was familiar with the verse in Ephesians 2:8–9: "For it is by grace you have been saved, through faith—and this not from yourselves, it is the gift of God—not by works, so that no one can boast." Somehow, though, I couldn't wrap my mind around the thought that such grace was for me. I felt broken beyond grace. Even though I was in church every Sunday, I started to rebel in my heart against God. The Devil had lied to me and convinced me that the condemnation, the self-loathing I felt were because I was an utter disappointment to God. Physically, I was in church, but emotionally, I started to disconnect and drift away.

Life with my husband had already become very coexistent. I was not feeling loved, desired, or valued. Mostly, I felt like the live-in cook and maid. Early on, I never talked to my husband about the way I was feeling. I grew up with the sense that my feelings didn't matter, and I believed that to be true. Avoiding conflict was another reason just to keep quiet about how I felt. I'm sure in my husband's mind he loved me and was trying his best to be a devoted, hard-working husband. But in my heart and mind I twisted it around, convincing myself that he in fact did not love me.

The old addictive behavior was starting to come back. Fact is, it never left. It just lay dormant for a while. It never left because I didn't understand what fueled it. I didn't even realize that an addictive pattern existed. All I knew was that I was terribly unhappy and I felt broken beyond repair. During this time I befriended a man who worked at a place beside my workplace, running into him on almost a daily basis. I'd look forward to seeing him because he reminded me a bit of my big brother with his free spirit. We also just seemed to click with our conversations, and he made me feel special. Our feelings of friendship toward one another started turning into feelings of desire. This confused me, being a married woman, and tormented my soul. It started me questioning why I was even married. I also hated myself even more, because what kind of Christian wife would have desires for another man?

I sought counsel from our pastor and prayed. I told my husband about it and ended my friendship with this other man. The Lord blessed me with a very patient and understanding husband. The Lord knew that I would need one. My husband and I worked on mending our relationship, and about a year later I became pregnant with our son. My pregnancy was a wonderful time in my life. Truly, I enjoyed being a part of the miracle of bringing another life into the world.

After having my son, however, instead of feeling closer to my husband, I felt even more distant. I remember resenting the fact that the day I came home with the baby, there was wash to be done and dinner to be cooked. Although I didn't open my mouth and ask for help, I resented my husband for not doing it. My mind told me that if I could see it needed to be done, he should also. I felt as though the total care of our son fell on me. The first three months were very hard. The baby was colicky, and I had postpartum depression. At night, I'd get next to no sleep because the baby was up every two to three hours. Many nights I'd just stay in the rocking chair, rocking the baby while I cried uncontrollably, resenting my husband all the more. Every time the baby would cry, I felt it was because of something I was doing wrong, leaving me once again to feel like a failure. For a year, I was treated with antidepressants, which didn't heal me, but made me care a bit less about the mental anguish I was in.

The more resentment I felt toward my husband over this time, the more I would cling to my son. He became my world—my only sense of happiness and fulfillment. Naturally, this caused a bit of jealousy on my husband's part, which in turn only made me resent him more. Remember, this was the man I expected to fix all my problems. Now I was starting to feel he was the cause of them. With each passing day, I emotionally detached from my husband more and more until I literally felt numb. I'd go through the days on autopilot. I'd get done what needed to get done but not fully participate in my life. I definitely was not participating in my marriage and did not even desire to try anymore. In my heart I had given up. It had become less painful for me just to give up than to feel that I was trying and failing.

As my son grew, I'd take the naughty little things he'd do in stride, but if he cried or whined, someplace deep inside of me erupted like a volcano. Rage like I had never experienced before came flowing out of me in the form of screaming and hate-filled words. Even though I had never felt myself get this way before, I recognized it. It was the same rage I used to see in my father's eyes and hear in his words. Now that rage was in me, and it scared me because I seemed to have no control over it. No doubt there were times I scared my son just as my dad used to scare me. This left me feeling horribly broken inside. It took me years to get a grip on this rage. There was so much pain stuffed deep inside of me that now it was boiling out of control. It needed to escape somehow.

To heal, I had to understand what triggered it. Many prayers for understanding and direction were lifted up and answered in God's perfect timing, not only my prayers but the prayers of faithful friends. I know now that my son's whining and crying triggered deep unresolved pain in me that went back through many years of feeling like a total failure because I couldn't fix the problems of people I loved. As a child I couldn't fix my parents problems and now I couldn't fix my son's. Years and years of frustration brewed and brewed until all my emotions reached a boiling point resulting in absolute rage. God is still trying to reveal to me that it's not up to me to fix them. It's up to Him. It is so very difficult to surrender these things to the Lord. But if you want to experience true healing, surrendering must be done.

CHAPTER EIGHT

Downward Spiral

By the time my son was two, all of the groundwork that fueled my addictive nature was in place again. I still battled with feelings of anger toward God and held on to resentment toward my husband to the point of emotionally disconnecting myself from him. I also became increasingly aware of each and every customer that I hadn't seen in a while, blaming myself if he or she didn't return even though I knew it was part of the business I was in. Still I internalized it as a rejection, basically confirming in my mind that I was a total screwup. I also harbored feelings of unforgiveness toward my parents and others I felt hurt by along the way, even though I had prayed many prayers of forgiveness for them. To add even more fuel to the fire, memories of my childhood were coming back to me now stronger than ever before. I later came to learn that memories of my childhood were triggered by my son. Often I would parallel my memories with how old he was at the time, remembering myself at his age. All these things once again added up to a deep, desperate pain and an enormous feeling of complete unworthiness. Somehow, someway, I just wanted the pain to stop.

Every time a man would compliment me, it would numb the deep-rooted pain. Slowly I started to seek after that attention and affirmation that anesthetized the pain, getting myself so wrapped up in the attention that many times things would spiral out of control, each time leaving me to feel even more self-hatred, which led into the need to seek out affirmation to feel better about myself. Countless friendships were destroyed in the process, each time sucking people into my madness only then to come to my senses and tell them just how inappropriate my actions and words had been. Even though I knew my behavior was sinful, it seemed I had no control over it. My need for love and acceptance had become a greater need than my desire to please God, even though it was my desire to please God that ultimately kept me from having a full-on affair with anyone. Thank God, literally, for that. I could so relate to Paul when he stated in Romans 7:15–25:

> "I do not understand what I do. For what I want to do I do not do, but what I hate I do, I agree that the law is good. As it is, it is no longer I myself who do it, but it is sin living in me. I know that nothing good lives in me, that is, in my sinful nature. For I have the desire to do what is good, but I can not carry it out. For what I do is not the good I want to do; no, the evil I do not want to do—this I keep on doing. Now if I do what I do not want to do, it is no longer I who do it, but it is sin living in me that does it. So I find this law at work. When I want to do good, evil is right there with me. For in my inner being I delight in God's law; but I see another law at work in the members of my body waging war against the law of my mind and making me a prisoner of the law of sin at work within my members. What a wretched man I am! Who will rescue me from this body of death? Thanks be to God—through Jesus Christ our Lord!"

Not only could I relate to this verse, but I gained comfort in the fact that I was and am not the only Christian to wrestle with a sinful nature. I also was comforted that I was not the only one who could feel two definite forces in my life, sometimes feeling like two separate people.

Every time I'd get my heart right with God and my focus on Him, it seemed Satan would set some kind of trap causing me to lose my focus on God, resulting in me stumbling again. Each time I was left to question how many times God was going to forgive me and how he could possibly love someone like me. Then God would lovingly direct me to Matthew 18:21–22: "Then Peter came to Jesus and asked 'Lord how many times should I forgive my brother when he sins against me? Up to seven times?' Jesus answered, 'I tell you not seven times but seventy-seven times.'" Then I'd pray earnestly for forgiveness and confess my sin as 1 John 1:9 says to do: "If we confess our sins, He is faithful and just and will forgive us our sins and cleanse us from all unrighteousness." Then I'd pray, "Dear Lord, will You somehow take what Satan meant for death and destruction and turn it into something that can be used for Your glory and benefit?" Through the years, God has been faithful in answering that prayer. He has certainly filled me with compassion for others that I don't think I'd have if it weren't for the many scrapes and bruises I've received along the road I have traveled.

Many prayers to God to fix me were lifted up. But time and time again, I'd take the reigns of my life back to try to fix myself instead of surrendering to Him. I just couldn't understand why I couldn't get a grip on this unacceptable behavior. If I was truly a child of God, why was I struggling with my sinful nature so much? The Lord pressed on my heart the need to find the source of my pain. That's when the process of me looking back on my past and childhood started. Many years have passed since I started this journey. The Lord has opened many doors for me to find the answers I've longed for. Some doors remain closed, but maybe someday God will choose to open them. I have learned that His timing is best. I've also learned to "Be joyful in hope, patient in affliction, faithful in prayer," as Romans 12:12 teaches.

Over these years, I sought the counsel of my pastor and a few different psychologists. Some counsel was Christian-based, other counsel was not. The conflicting opinions of the two left me utterly confused, causing me to seek counsel through the writings of Christian authors, much of which I did find extremely helpful. The non-Christian counsel would guide me to follow my heart and go after the things I felt would make me happy, buying into the modern-day, new-age belief that everyone deserves to be happy. It taught the relative philosophy that what is right for one person may not be right for the next and what is wrong for one may not be wrong for the other. God protected my mind so I didn't get sucked into this harmful way of thinking. There are absolute truths. They are in the Bible. Yes, I wanted desperately to be happy, but I did not want to disobey my Lord to follow my own happiness. As screwed up as I was at that point, I knew enough that my Lord's plan for me was good and perfect, not the plan I had made up in my head. Some of the Christian counsel I did receive was helpful but not the easy fix I was searching for at that point. Nothing worth it is ever easy. If healing, inner peace, and joy are worth it, then you need to commit yourself to the work it takes to get there. Give yourself time to go through the process to heal. Place enough value in yourself to seek after that healing.

During these years of deep emotional battles and mental torment over my longing for love, I was diagnosed with a tumor adjacent to my right kidney. Blood work and a CAT scan–guided biopsy were inconclusive as to whether this tumor was malignant or benign. The next step was to go in for surgery. The doctor informed me that the first step after opening me up would be to take a sample of the tumor and run a pathology report on it. If it came back benign, they would remove the tumor. If it came back malignant, the tumor would have to stay due to the risk of causing the cancer to travel if they tried to remove it. So I had no idea what kind of news I would hear when I woke up. This was a very trying time for me, and I wanted reassuring comfort from my husband, but he did not know how to show that to me.

Thankfully, the tumor was benign and so it was removed. That should have been it. I should have been able to go back to being the strong, vibrant healthy woman I was before, but that's not what happened. While still in recovery in the hospital after my surgery, I felt an enormous amount of pain—much more than I felt I should have. Yes, abdominal surgeries are extremely painful, but something just felt wrong to me. My blood pressure also elevated with each passing day instead of going down to normal. A normal blood pressure for me at that time was usually around 110 over 60, so when my blood pressure the day after surgery was 120 over 70, no one, including myself, was alarmed. However, the next day it had gone up to 130 over 90. Now this was alarming to me and also to my mother, who had come to support me through this. We questioned the nurse but got back a very stern order to "calm down!" She somewhat yelled at me, stating that the only reason my blood pressure was elevated was because I was anxious to get home and that I needed to calm myself down. When the doctor was questioned, he didn't seem to be alarmed by it either.

After being released from the hospital, I still felt a lot of pain, not just from the surgical sight, but deep within. They were throbbing and sometimes very sharp shooting pains. Along with that, I was getting shakes and chills, and I seemed to catch every cold and virus known to man. Four months after the surgery I went to my ob-gyn for a routine physical. When the nurse took my blood pressure, she looked at me and asked, "Ali, have you been feeling alright?" I replied, "No, I've been sick ever since my surgery four months ago." She continued to tell me that my blood pressure was 130 over 90 and that it was quite abnormal for me. I commented, "Yes, that is what it was in the hospital, and I thought it to be unusual at that time as well." The doctor then agreed with the nurse that I should start having this matter checked, so she advised me to see my regular doctor as soon as possible. Two weeks later, I was sitting in my doctor's office, and both the doctor and nurse looked at me with some concern and alarm as they retook my blood pressure. The numbers matched the reading of the blood pressure they had just taken, 150 over 100. No doubt, this was a problem. Then a million and one questions started. Each time I'd say, "This did not start until my surgery." But each time that was passed off as a possible contributing factor. In the weeks that followed, I went for blood work, CAT scans, MRIs, ultrasounds, EKGs, and a few other tests of which I don't even recall the names. Something was wrong, and no one could find any answers to give me.

Let me pause for a moment here to fill you in on what was going on with me emotionally. I had a fairly new business that I co-owned but felt responsible to keep up with, a now four-year-old son who needed his mommy, and a house to take care of inside and out. After my surgery, I would try to get my husband to understand how physically drained I felt, how much pain I was in, and how much I questioned why I was getting sick so often. I'd keep telling him that something was wrong. His reaction to me made me feel as though I was just complaining and overreacting; it even somewhat made me feel that I was crazy. One thing I didn't feel was supported. So once again I just shut down. It got to the point that I didn't want to share anything with him because when I did, I just felt stupid for doing so.

After my family doctor ordered and ran all the tests he could possibly think of, he sent me to a kidney specialist. The tumor I had was adjacent to my right kidney, and now he was starting to believe that the blood pressure elevation and illnesses may in fact have been linked to the first surgery. Within a week after getting referred to the kidney specialist, I was sitting in his office. Now anyone that has had to see a specialist before knows that it usually takes months to get in. I was seen only after a week of being referred. That's just plain scary. What was even scarier was the fact that by the time I got to his office my blood pressure was 170 over 100. Much higher and I'd be a candidate for a stroke. Immediately I was put on blood pressure medication, which is completely laughable for someone who has had problems with low blood pressure her whole life.

The kidney specialist ordered a renal angiogram for me. Within a few days I was in the hospital for the procedure. I will never forget that day or the absolute sweet honesty that came from that doctor's lips. I was awake for the procedure and the doctor was just around the other side of the room from me behind the partition when I heard him exclaim, "Those idiots crushed her renal artery." There was no doubt now what had been going on with me. The doctor then came around to my side and said, "Sweetheart, I don't know how to tell you this, but apparently when they were removing your tumor, your renal artery got crushed." He went on to explain that I was one of those very few people who had a second small vein supplying blood to the kidney. That's why it didn't just die off. It was being fed just enough blood to be kept alive but was under such distress that many, many, toxins were getting into my bloodstream and pumped all over my body. That's why my blood pressure was elevated, and that's why my immune system was so battered.

A very short time after finding that out, my right kidney was removed. Each and every day after that I got stronger and healthier. The nightmare was over. Well, at least physically it was, but emotionally this had taken quite a toll. If I hadn't closed my heart off to my husband before, well I certainly did now. Instead of seeking him for comfort I looked for other ways to make myself feel stronger. To give myself a sense of fighting back from all that had happened, I turned to running. Kind of like Forrest Gump in the movie, I started running and couldn't stop. It made me feel stronger and was an outlet for all the inner pain I felt. The one-year anniversary of my kidney removal was celebrated with my first 5k run. Joy permeated every ounce of my being as I crossed that finish line. Short of giving birth, I had never felt so utterly exhilarated in my life. I continued to chase after that exhilaration. Race after race, I increased the number of miles with each one, having the mindset to better myself with each step I took. What started with a 5k eventually took me all the way to running in my first marathon for the Leukemia and Lymphoma Society. What an honor and a privilege this was for me. Not only did the running make me feel physically and emotionally stronger but now I had joy in knowing I was helping others through my running. Yes, the Lord was showering tremendous blessing down on me over this time. My husband was also being very supportive of my running, which began to touch my heart.

There came a point though that I had to realize that I was running away from all my problems and that I had to stop running and face them. So after years of running many races, marathons, and ultras, I slowed down. I still run but now for just the enjoyment of it, not in response to a mad driving force as if my very life depended on it. I must thank my Lord, however, for the gift of running; it did truly set my feet on a path back to Him. For this I am eternally grateful. It gave me a source of well-being and of personal strength and achievement. It was something I could like, if not love, about myself. What a blessing that has been to me.

CHAPTER NINE

A Long Road to Healing

ONE OF THE first steps to healing that I had to take was a journey back in time. I prayed that God would reveal to me the things I needed to remember in order to learn from them and move on. The long path to healing involved not only self-discovery but also the discovery of who my parents were as ordinary people and the hurdles they had to overcome from their childhood and lives. My mother grew up in a large family with a physically abusive father and a mother who had abandoned them all. My mother was left with deep emotional scars. By the time my dad showed up in my mom's late teens, she was itching for a way to get out of her abusive home. After a very short time of knowing each other, my father asked my mom to go to California with him, which was where he was to be stationed in the army. She replied, "I do hope you mean married." So they wed even though they barely knew each other.

My father doesn't have any memories of his mother because she died of pneumonia when he was very young. His father, unable to care for his needs, brought him to a couple he knew. They lived on a beautiful farm hours away, the farm that we eventually moved to when I was ten. Although undoubtedly this older couple took wonderful care of him, I am sure he grew up feeling much like a hired farm hand. I bet he felt abandoned by both his mother and father, even though his dad would visit from time to time.

So both parents grew up with abandonment issues. Neither knew unconditional love, and I'm certain they built many walls around their emotions as protective coverings. Both, I believe, tried to do their best in raising their children. What often happens, however, is that children become products of their parents' unhealed past. It has become so very important to me to understand it all so I can break the chains and the unhealthy patterns of the unhealed hearts of past generations, including my own. The last thing in the world I want to do is pass all this heartache and baggage along to my son. No, it needs to stop and end with me.

Trying to look at my parents as just people who had great hurdles and hardships of their own has taken the focus off me. This is a good thing, because it's not "all about me." It has allowed me to understand in a more compassionate way that they have healing to do as well. As an adult I have the choice either to allow my past to consume and dominate me in darkness or break out of that darkness, learn from my past, and, with God's help, heal and move forward in a positive light. To escape darkness, one must be willing to step into the light. You must be willing to deal with whatever the light (the truth) may reveal. Isn't it better to live a life of freedom, not being trapped in a pit, than to live a life weighted down and consumed by the darkness within? Pray for strength and encouragement to step out of the dark and into the light. The Lord will be faithful and true in blessing and answering that prayer.

The childhood memories I shared in the beginning of this book were the doors the Lord opened to me, leading me to understand the things that lay the foundation for self-hatred and unhealthy thought processing and also softening my heart to forgive everyone involved, including myself. He also blessed me with being able to restore many friendships along the way, especially those from my youth. It's been an amazing and marvelous journey, although sometimes quite painful. Reconnecting with people from my past helped teach me about the Ali I left behind. I was able to see that the Ali of yesteryear was worthy of love as much as the Ali of today. Self-hatred through the years clouded my view of just how people from my past thought of me. It's amazing how when you hate yourself, you think that everyone else must have felt the same way about you. Now I know that was not true at all. The realization that I was actually liked back then has brought me tremendous peace and healing.

It's been two years since I started the process of reconnecting with my past. The feeling of disconnect inside of me between the Ali of my youth and the adult Ali have started to merge now into one complete Ali. That is a true gift from God, giving me a sense of wholeness now. The Lord is still healing me from a sense of lost youth. It's hard for me at times to look back without questioning what would things have been like if I hadn't been such a wounded spirit. But I know I'm who I am today because of the road I've traveled. Hopefully, God can use me to bless someone's life that only I can because I've been there too. I'm actually grateful for the lessons I have learned over the years of coming to terms with my past. The Lord is able to use this healing in marvelous ways. I've seen Him do it.

God has brought true healing to me regarding my youth. Now when traveling back to my childhood home, I can marvel in the beauty of the area and feel no pain. All I feel is blessed to have grown up in an area as lovely as the one I did. Now I can enjoy seeing people from my past and remember good times instead of painful memories. I've also been able to ask forgiveness from some I may have hurt along the way and have received it. The more I surrender to God and place in his hands the more blessings I receive. He has blessed me with a patient, faithful, and loving husband and a beyond-words-awesome son. The Lord is good!

As I stated in the beginning, God is far from finished with me. I've had to accept that I am most definitely a work in progress. I still need to surround myself with other Christian believers, those who will hold me accountable but who will also lift me up in prayer. The Lord has surrounded me with valued friends who will share in my victories, but will be there to help lift me out of the pits. If I had things my way, God would have instantly healed me from this nasty addictive behavior. Instead I have learned that I need to walk closely with God each and every day so I do not stumble and fall. The Lord has brought me amazing peace and a heart filled with love in the process. He's brought unimaginable healing to me by love shown to me now by both people from my past and present. The most amazing gift to me is now I'm able to accept that love. Finally I've accepted that God can love someone like me. I know that I am far from perfect, but I also know God created me and I am beautiful in His sight. Inner healing has brought me to the point of being able now to love myself "warts and all." Now that I have love for myself, I can accept the love of others and love them back in return.

Over the last couple years, the Lord has also brought great healing to my marriage. He has given me a voice to discuss my hurts, dreams, and desires with my husband and has given him a desire to listen and support me. It has also taught me that my husband has thoughts, dreams, and desires of his own. I am to be there to support him in the same way that I desire him to support me. That has been a tremendous gift. Marriage is a gift, but one that you don't just open one day and cast aside the next. No, this gift takes much commitment, care, and nurturing. We sought help through Christian counseling for a time to help establish open lines of communication for us. Communication is the key. Don't be afraid to seek Christian counsel. God works through His children. Sometimes we just pray for healing but don't allow God to bring us that healing through those around us.

My past can now stay in the past, although I am totally excited to bring along some of the people from my past into my brightened future. There may still be a few roadblocks along the way, but now I am excited to see just how God will move those roadblocks and lead me around the bends.

It says in Hebrews 12:1, "Let us throw off everything that hinders and the sin that so easily entangles, and let us run with perseverance the race marked out for us." I'm ready now, with God's help, to run with perseverance this race called life.

EPILOGUE

I find myself writing this epilogue more than a year after finishing this book. You may have been led to believe at the end of Chapter Nine that my life was going to be a smooth upward rise to eternal peace and happiness. Instead, my Christian walk has been one of many stubbed toes, ankle twists, and falls causing me to lift my head upward and gain the strength to rise to my feet once again. At one point I would experience moments of temporary, illuminating peace and security, but it was often followed by downward spirals into places of utter darkness.

It is true of Scripture that when people come to accept Christ as their Lord and Savior, "They are a new creation, the old has gone, the new has come!" as 2 Corinthians 5:17 states. However, it has been my personal experience that it is very hard to stay on top of that mountain. Many times we fall down and struggle to regain footing to climb back up, often lacking the energy to do so. At times we stumble so far back that before we know it, we are in a pit, seemingly trapped in the depths of darkness.

Writing this book, I admit, may be a form of self-therapy. It has truly helped me get all my thoughts out and down on paper. I encourage anyone who is struggling to do the same. Journal and get your thoughts out instead of harboring them inside. Though writing this has helped me personally, I pray even more that it will help others realize they are not alone in their struggles.

Many Christians have experienced tremendous born-again transformations of their minds, hearts, and souls, leading them on what seems to be a stable and steady path always upward to becoming more Christlike. Others are left questioning, sometimes daily, "Am I really a Christian? How can I possibly be a child of God if I think or feel this way?" Always remember, dear child of the risen King, that you are loved. Hold on to that truth and remind yourself of it often. Christ died for you. Not just for me. Not only for him or her, but also for you!

To escape darkness, it is my belief that you not only have to understand what created it, but you also must grasp fully how to shine light into all the corners, nooks, and crannies to completely abolish it. Webster's dictionary defines *dark* as "entirely or partly without light, almost black, not light in color, hidden, gloomy, evil, sinister, ignorant." My heart, mind, and very soul have at one time or another been very *dark*. I understand and agree with Webster's definition and have decided that I don't want my picture to be there in the dictionary beside that word. I'd much rather have my photo beside *light*. Among the many definitions Webster's has for it, my favorites are, "to set on fire, ignite, to cause to give off light." That's just what the Lord does for us when we surrender to Him and ask Jesus into our hearts. True, we can allow darkness to cover over us and dim that light in us, but the light is still there. Call on God and trust in Him, He is still there. Light, as also defined by Webster's, means "having little weight." That's what Christ will do when you step out of the darkness and into the light. He will make the trash you've been carrying around "light."

From childhood on into my adult years, it has been an ongoing struggle to combat the darkness in my mind, heart, and soul, and at times I was utterly consumed by it. I was in utter despair and depressed. A long family history of depression and mental illness exists. Although part of me believes that adds to the inner battles, greater though is my belief that there is a spiritual battle waging in my soul. The apostle Paul speaks of it in Romans 7:14–25: "We know that the law is spiritual; but I am unspiritual, sold as a slave to sin." He continues on to say, "I do not understand what I do. For what I want to do I do not do, but what I hate I do." This is where Satan has not only gotten a foothold over me but a stronghold over my mind. This is the source of darkness in my life—the deep, dark pit of despair that has become an ongoing struggle. Oh, how I long to be clothed in righteousness, to be all that my Lord has created me to be. I earnestly and desperately want to be holy and pure, but at times I willfully live the complete opposite way. I feel trapped in a longing to be one way, but think, feel, and act another. How absolutely maddening it is, especially when you seem utterly powerless to change it. You do not even know how to surrender it all to God so He can change it—so He can change me. Have you ever felt this way?

Has Satan ever had such a foothold over you that you continually feel as though you need to rededicate your life to the Lord because obviously the first, second, or third time didn't work? Do you feel that you somehow must have said or done something wrong when you asked Jesus into your heart? Maybe you didn't mean it enough. You had to have done something wrong because you still feel trapped in sin. You still feel unworthy, unlovely, unholy, and unacceptable. My dear one, you are not alone. I know these dark struggles and the torture they can bring if you allow Satan to keep you trapped in them. Don't resolve to stay in the pit with the deceiver. Fight back and ask the Lord to throw you a ladder or rope so you can climb out. Better yet, reach up your hands and allow Him to pull you out. You may feel as if you don't deserve His help, but He wants to give it to you. You may feel as though you don't deserve His love, but He wants to lavish His love upon you. All you need to do is ask for and accept His help. Accept His love. Don't allow the Devil to convince you that you are stuck there and will never get out. God does not want us to stay in the darkness of the holes we have dug for ourselves. He wants to pull us out, but we need to allow Him to do that. Remember, He has given us free will. We can either choose to wallow in the darkness or we can choose to allow Him to set us free. *Choose freedom!* With each dawning of a new day comes a choice. You can either live trapped in pains from past mistakes or tragedies, or you can boldly claim God's gift of a new start. Some of us have to claim that new start with each new sunrise.

Sunrises have become such a cherished and sought-after splendor for me. When a new day dawns, the most beautiful colors paint the sky. Breaking through the darkness, a sunrise creates the most spectacular light show of magical yellows, oranges, pinks, and blues. Think about it. Is the sky that lovely in the full light of day? Yes, of course you can have a gorgeous day, but are the colors nearly as pretty as they are when contrasted against a darkened sky? Whether it be a sunrise or sunset, the boldest array of color comes out of the darkness. Just look at how brilliantly the stars shine against a backdrop of darkness at night.

If you wonder how God could possibly love you or use you, if you feel consumed by darkness, just think of what beauty can flow out of that darkness if you just allow God's light to illuminate through you. Just like a sunrise, out of darkness beauty can flow. For God said in 2 Corinthians 4:5, "Let light shine out of darkness." Allow yourself to accept the notion that the Lord can bring great beauty from that darkness within you when you allow Him to shine through.

Never lose hope! Second Corinthians 4:16 says, "Therefore we do not lose heart." It continues on, "Though outwardly we are wasting away, yet inwardly we are being renewed day by day. For our light and momentary troubles are achieving for us an eternal glory that far outweighs them all." Did you catch the part "outwardly we are wasting away"? Consider this for a moment. A sugar maple emits bright vivid colors as it "outwardly wastes away." In the coolness of autumn, under the bright shining sun, the sugar maple explodes in colors just as it is "wasting away," losing one leaf after another, leaving the tree utterly leafless and looking dead. But it is not dead. It is being renewed and will burst forth into new life in the spring. So it is for our souls. In times of darkness, it may feel as though we are "wasting away." In a spiritual way, we are dying to self. But we are being renewed in our spirits to be even more alive in Christ. So embrace God's light and renewing spirit in times of darkness. Also rejoice in the beautiful colors He will create in you and shine from within you. Yes, we will have elating ups and heart-wrenching downs. But keep your focus on God and His light. Hold onto hope that God is able to use the downs to create even more beauty in us than we could have ever imagined. As it says in 2 Corinthians 4:16, "Yet outwardly we are being renewed day by day."

So get out there, dear friend, and let God's light shine through you, blessing all who see the beautiful array of colors that He will bring forth from your life. For it is the dawning of a new day—the sunrise of your soul. Get out there and glory in the beauty that God is creating in you. You are "a new creation." Each and every dawning of a new day, "the old has gone, the new has come"!

NOTES

All biblical references are taken from the NIV translation.

Books that helped me understand my emotions, struggles, and addictive patterns:

Anderson, Neil T., and Mike Quarles. *Overcoming Addictive Behavior.* Ventura, CA: Regal Books, 2003.
O'Neill, Cherry and Dan. *Living on the Border of Disorder.* Bloomington, MN: Bethany House Publishers, 1992.
Seamonds, David A. *Healing for Damaged Emotions.* Colorado Springs, CO: David C. Cook, 1981.